Discovering

DAMSELFLIES AND DRAGONFLIES

Linda Losito

The Bookwright Press
New York · 1988

Discovering Nature

Further titles are in preparation

All photographs from Oxford Scientific Films

Cover *Adult damselflies are usually smaller and more slender than dragonflies.*

Frontispiece *Dragonflies are much stronger faster fliers than damselflies.*

First published in the
United States in 1988 by
The Bookwright Press
387 Park Avenue South
New York, NY 10016

First published in 1987 by
Wayland (Publishers) Limited
61 Western Road, Hove
East Sussex BN3 1JD, England

ISBN 0-531-18168-5

Library of Congress Catalog Card Number: 87-71047

Typeset by DP Press Ltd., Sevenoaks, Kent
Printed in Italy by Sagdos S.p.A., Milan

Contents

1
Introducing Damselflies and Dragonflies

Dragonflies have quite stout bodies. They rest with their wings open like this.

Damselflies and dragonflies are brightly colored insects often seen darting about near ponds and streams. They are not true flies because they have two pairs of wings instead of one. They belong to a group of insects called *Odonata*, a Greek word that means having teeth.

In the past, some grew to an enormous size, with a wingspan of 75 cm (29 in). Their **fossils** are sometimes found in coal beds. The coal was formed from the ancient forests in which the damselflies and dragonflies flew.

Today, they are much smaller, although some giant kinds have a wingspan of 18 cm (7 in). The design of their bodies has hardly changed at all. There are at least 5,000 different kinds, and most of them live in countries with warm climates.

Like all insects, they have their skeletons on the outside of the body.

It is called an **exoskeleton** and is made of a light horny material called chitin (kite-in). It has an outer waterproof covering of wax. The insects breathe through tiny openings in the exoskeleton called **spiracles**.

The body has three parts called the

This dragonfly lived 110 million years ago. It had a wingspan of 85mm (3 in).

head, **thorax** and **abdomen**. The four wings and six legs are joined onto the thorax. The head bears a pair of large **compound eyes** and two **antennae**.

Adult damselflies are usually smaller and more slender than dragonflies. All four of their wings are a similar paddle shape. When at rest, the insect folds them neatly over its body. A dragonfly's hindwings are much broader than its front wings. The resting insect holds its wings away from the body. Dragonflies are much stronger, faster fliers than damselflies. They are often found far away from water, even in deserts.

Both types of insects are hunters. Their large eyes can pick up the slightest movement. The mobile head can be turned in any direction. The eyes of dragonflies are very close together on the front of the head. A damselfly's eyes are farther apart on the sides of its head.

Damselflies have very slender bodies. Unlike dragonflies they rest with their wings raised.

The eyes of a damselfly are on the sides of the head.

A dragonfly's eyes are at the front of the head. They meet in the middle.

The compound eyes are made of thousands of separate sections called **facets**. This gives the surface of the eye a net-like appearance. Some kinds of dragonflies have larger facets in the upper half of the eye. These are good for seeing moving objects. The smaller facets in the lower half of the eye are better for seeing things that are not moving. Insects that fly at night or at dusk have especially large eyes.

The eyes are kept clean with special combs on the insect's front legs. Some damselflies and dragonflies even wash their eyes with drops of water collected in their mouths.

2
Adult Life

A damselfly eating a moth that it has caught on the wing.

Hunting on the Wing

Damselflies and dragonflies catch their prey while in flight. The two pairs of wings can beat separately from each other because the flight muscles are joined to the base of the wings. (The flight muscles of other insects are joined to the exoskeleton.) They are dazzling acrobats in the air, able to swoop low, turn sharply and even fly backward. Some of the larger dragonflies can reach speeds of over 30 kph (19 mph).

Damselflies and dragonflies have long legs that can be used for perching on twigs, but not for walking. The thorax is tilted so that the legs point forward. They are held together to form a net for catching insects. They have many bristles, which give a good grip. Large numbers of flies, beetles and mosquitos are trapped in midair. The insects often follow horses or cows to catch the many flies that swarm around them. They will also catch bugs and spiders from the surface of plants. They chew the prey using strong jaws. The tough parts like legs and wings are discarded. Sometimes they kill more insects than they can eat.

A giant damselfly that lives in South America has a special way of feeding. It dashes through spiders' webs and steals their prey. Some dragonflies may eat small frogs.

Above *The bristles on a dragonfly's legs are useful for trapping small insects.*

Left *A damselfly feeding on the soft parts of a cranefly. The tough legs are discarded.*

Temperature control

Dragonflies and damselflies are cold-blooded. This means that they cannot control their body temperature from inside. At rest, their temperature is the same as their surroundings. On a cold day they may not have enough energy to move. This can be a problem for insects living in colder climates. They cope with this problem in several ways. Active muscles make heat, so the insects warm up by beating their wings. They are then warm enough to fly. If they sit in warm sunny spots with their wings spread out, they pick up heat from sunlight. They often land on pale surfaces like bare rock. These reflect more sunlight than dark surfaces.

In hot climates their body temperature may rise too high. Many kinds keep cool by flying only at dawn or dusk when the temperature is

A damselfly raises its abdomen to keep from becoming too hot in direct sunlight.

lower. A very few fly only at night because they hunt by sight. During the day, they rest in dark shaded places. Some daytime fliers rest with their abdomens pointing straight upward. The body temperature does not rise too much because less sunlight falls on the abdomen. The

Two male damselflies sit on a pale rock surface in sunlight. They are warming up before take-off.

wings are spread out to shade the thorax. On the hottest days, they prefer to fly in cool shaded places like woodland.

Color Changes

When they first emerge, adult damselflies and dragonflies are a pale fawn color. Their bright colors take time to develop. Males and females of the same kind often look quite different when their colors are established.

The blue color of this dragonfly is caused by a powdery surface layer of pigment on the skin.

The colors are formed in several different ways. Some insects have color chemicals or pigments in a fatty layer under the skin. They show through the clear layers above them. When the insect dies, the fat breaks down and the colors disappear.

The metallic colors do not fade after death. They are caused almost the same way a rainbow's colors are caused. Light is scattered by structures in the skin, making the insects look green, blue or violet.

A third type of color develops on the skin surface. It is a powdery layer like the "bloom" on a grape. Dull brown males can change to a dazzling blue in a very short time.

As they age, damselflies and dragonflies may pass through several color changes, from pink through emerald green to blue. The wings, legs and eyes also change. Some adults have bright blue bands on their wings.

Above *A male dragonfly from Sarawak.*

Left *Pale, freshly emerged damselflies. They will be bright blue when mature.*

Damselflies and dragonflies that live in cooler northern areas tend to be darker than southern forms. This is because dark colors warm up more quickly than pale colors, so they can begin hunting for food earlier in the day.

Securing a Territory

Male dragonflies become adult before the females. Some kinds set up territories, which they guard against other males. This is to provide a protected place for the females to lay eggs after **mating**. It is usually part of a sunny, weedy pond or stream with clean water. A few special types use water-filled holes in trees.

The males sit on a branch or plant stem and watch over the territory. Larger, fiercer males usually have bigger territories than the smaller ones. Male damselflies often do not have territories at all.

Some male dragonflies fight with an intruder by butting him from beneath. The intruder tries to fly underneath him and they spin down to the water surface. The loser may drown or be eaten by a fish. Usually, he flies off to form a new territory somewhere else.

A male dragonfly sits on a twig and watches over his territory.

He may not mate without a territory.

Different kinds of damselflies and dragonflies do battle by flashing colors at each other. They may display colored legs or wings, or raise a bright abdomen. The male that makes the best display keeps the territory. Complicated circular or zig-zag dances are also used to see which male is the stronger.

The males usually fight in the late morning when it is warmer. On cold days they hardly move at all.

Male dragonflies threaten each other by raising the abdomen.

Courting and Mating

Male damselflies and dragonflies must now find the right kind of female to mate with. He recognizes her by the size, shape and color of her body and wings. In some kinds, the way the female flies is important. The male is not attracted if she is sitting still.

If a male chooses the wrong kind of female, all his effort is wasted. The female's eggs will not hatch. Most males grab the first female that seems right. They can sometimes make mistakes and grab other males.

Some types of male dragonflies attract a female by making a colorful display. One curves his abdomen forward to show off his scarlet back. Another dangles his white legs in front of the female. She may go into a sort of trance. Some males circle over

A male and female damselfly about to mate.

the water, flashing bright wings in a special dance. They show off the egg-laying site to the female.

Once a mate has been chosen, the male picks up the female with his **claspers**. These are at the tip of the abdomen. Dragonfly males hold their

Some males attract a mate by displaying their white legs.

mates by the head. Male damselflies grasp the female around the front of the thorax. Damselflies do not usually perform **courtship** displays.

A pair of damselflies resting in the tandem position.

These emerald damselflies are mating in the wheel position.

Male dragonflies and damselflies make **sperm** in sex organs near the tip of the abdomen. The males cannot mate with these organs because they need the tip to hold the female. Instead, they use a structure called a secondary sex organ, in which sperm is stored, to fertilize the female's eggs.

The male curls the tip of the abdomen under his body and deposits a packet of sperm into a special pocket.

Mating can take a few seconds or several hours. Short matings take place in flight, usually over water. Longer matings occur while the pair is perched, often away from water.

At first the female is carried **in tandem** with her abdomen trailing out behind. Then she curves her body forward beneath the male. Her sex organs connect with the male's secondary sex organs. Sometimes the male persuades the female to do this by stroking her with his legs.

The male may have a special structure attached to his sex organs. He uses this to scrape the sperm of other males out of the female and replace it with his own sperm. Then his sperm will join with and fertilize the female's eggs.

The male damselfly has lowered his wings to warn off any intruding males while he is mating.

Laying Eggs Underwater

The female usually lays her eggs right after mating. They pass from her body through an egg-laying tube or **ovipositor**. This is at the tip of the abdomen.

The male often stays with the female to guard her from other males and to make sure that her eggs have been fertilized only by his sperm.

Some males just fly close beside the female. Others hold onto her with claspers. They fly in tandem down to the surface of the water.

Different kinds of females have different ways of laying eggs. Some drop them directly into the water. These eggs are smooth and rounded.

This damselfly male holds onto his mate while she lays her eggs in the water.

This female damselfly is laying eggs in an underwater plant stem. She breathes oxygen from the silvery envelope of air.

Other females inject their eggs into plants. These eggs are longer, with pointed ends.

The females may scatter their eggs on the water. They sink down to the bottom of the pond. Many eggs will be eaten by fish. Other females dip their ovipositor below the surface. The eggs drop to the bottom faster but the dragonflies risk being eaten by fish themselves. A third type clambers with a male down a plant stem deep into the water. They take a bubble of air for breathing. They may both stay underwater for up to an hour. The eggs are injected into the base of the stem. Here they are protected from fish and other **predators**.

Laying Eggs on Land

Many females leave the male when mating is over. They may be pounced on by other males. They can show they are not ready to mate by raising their wings and abdomen. The males go off in search of an unmated female.

The female uses her large eyes to select the right egg-laying site. Those that lay in tree leaves must find a branch hanging over water. When the **larvae** hatch out, they drop straight

A female damselfly lays her eggs in the stem of a plant.

into the water. If eggs are laid on the ground, they must be protected from drying out. Some eggs are round so they roll into damp hollows.

Females that lay eggs in plants have a tiny saw-like structure on the ovipositor. This is for cutting through the tough plant surface. Some females are very particular about which kind of plant they use. Others are less choosy. They try to make sure not to lay too many eggs in the same place. Overcrowding can kill the young through lack of food and oxygen. Also, the plant may die.

Some dragonfly females damage their wings during egg-laying, and they soon die. Others mate a second time and lay another batch of eggs. At the end of the mating season, all the adults die. Only the young survive.

Above *These females are laying their eggs in a water-logged branch.*

Left *Some female dragonflies drop their eggs into the water from the air.*

3
Larvae and Young Adults

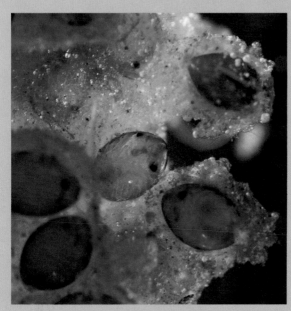

Look closely at this batch of dragonfly eggs. You can see the eyes of the larvae through the shells.

Growing Up Underwater

Some kinds of eggs lie dormant for several months before hatching. Others may hatch within two weeks. A tiny worm-like creature called a pro-larva emerges. It molts or changes its skin almost immediately to become a first **instar** larva.

Adult damselflies and dragonflies do not emerge from a **pupa** like butterflies. Instead, the larva gradually changes to look more like the adult. It may change its skin up to fifteen times. The larva can only grow when it has a new soft skin. Tiny wing buds appear on the back in the later stages. The eyes get bigger and cover more of the head. The adult emerges from the skin of the final instar.

Damselfly larvae have slender bodies with three leaf-like **gills** at the tip of the abdomen. They take in

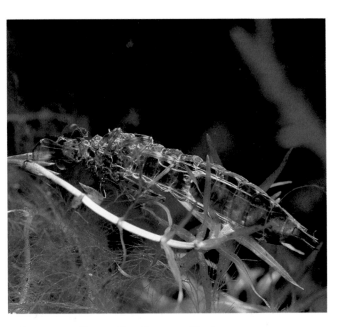

The cast skin of a dragonfly larva.

bottom. Some hide in burrows in the mud. They poke the tip of the abdomen out to take oxygen in through a **siphon**.

Beneath the head of this dragonfly larva you can see a spiny mask.

oxygen from the water with these gills. Dragonfly larvae are stouter, and have five spines at the tip. They take in oxygen through gills in the **rectum**. The insect uses muscles to pump water in and out of the rectum.

The larvae are either green or a muddy-brown color. They are well hidden among weeds or on the pond

Newly hatched larvae feed on the yolk inside their bodies. Older larvae catch and eat other creatures. They will eat worms, tadpoles, small fish and the larvae of other insects. They may even eat their own kind.

Larvae that live in murky water use their antennae to find prey. Other

A damselfly larva, showing the three leaf-like gills at the tip of the abdomen.

kinds use their well-developed eyes. They trap the prey with a special part of the jaw called the mask. It has sharp hooks and spines, and lies beneath the mouth. It is pumped up

This dragonfly larva has caught a tadpole with the mask. It will now be pulled into the mouth.

with blood and shoots forward at great speed. The prey is drawn into the mouth to be eaten.

The larvae stalk their prey by creeping toward it so slowly they hardly seem to be moving. If they are being hunted themselves, they can move much faster. Damselfly larvae swim by bending the whole body from side to side. Dragonfly larvae move by forcing a jet of water out of the rectum, which pushes them rapidly forward.

Some larvae develop into adults in only thirty days. These live in temporary pools, which soon dry up in hot climates. Other kinds may take five or six years to develop. They usually live in cooler places where food is less plentiful.

The adult dragonfly breaks out of the larval skin and hangs upside down.

Moving Out of the Water

A fully developed larva moves from cool deep water into warmer shallow water. This takes it to the edge of the pond or stream. It stops feeding and the mouthparts begin to change. It climbs out of the water up a plant stem. Some larvae have been found climbing the sides of boats or wooden posts. This usually occurs at night in warmer climates. In cooler areas it takes place just after sunrise.

Once in the air, the larva grasps the stem very tightly with its legs. After a short rest it begins to wriggle. The larval skin splits just behind the head. Inside is the adult insect. It thrusts its head and thorax through the split. Now it hangs upside down until the new skin has dried and hardened. After a few hours, it jerks itself forward and grips the old skin. The rest of the abdomen is pulled free.

A freshly emerged damselfly sitting on its old larval skin while it dries.

Blood is pumped into the soft crumpled wings. These gradually unfold, dry and harden in the warm air. Finally the abdomen fills out. It changes from the fat larval shape to the tube-like adult form. The insect hangs from its old skin until it is warmed by the sun. It then takes off on its first flight.

The emerging adult dragonfly then holds onto the larval skin while it pulls out the rest of its body.

Adult Damselflies and Dragonflies

Newly emerged adult damselflies and dragonflies fly away from the water. They find a perch and rest for ten to twelve hours while their skin and wings harden. They only return to water to breed, staying away from a few days to weeks. During this time they feed and the organs that make eggs and sperm develop. The brilliant adult colors appear. Some tropical insects become mature only in the rainy season.

The adults have a very short life-span. The damselflies may live for one or two weeks. Dragonflies may live a week or two longer. Older insects of six or eight weeks have been known. They often have frayed battered wings. Some damage is caused when males fight over their territories.

Adult damselflies and dragonflies carry a number of **parasites**, which may weaken them. A wingless parasitic fly lives on the insects' wings. It sucks blood from the wing veins. Tiny spider-like mites live in crevices on the abdomen and thorax.

An old female dragonfly. Her wings are frayed.

They are also bloodsuckers.

Another parasite, a kind of worm, is more harmful to the birds that eat the insects. It breaks through the bird's gut, and causes damage to the

A fresh, brightly colored damselfly male resting on a flower.

inside organs, which keeps the bird from laying many eggs.

4
Enemies and Other Dangers

As this damselfly lays her eggs, a fish lies in wait to eat them.

Enemies of Eggs and Larvae

Although damselflies and dragonflies lay millions of eggs, very few turn into adults. If too many survived, they would die of starvation. Also they provide other creatures with food.

When the female is laying her eggs, she is in great danger. Frogs, fish, insects and spiders are waiting to snap her up. Surface-feeding insects, like the water-boatman, will attack any damselflies or dragonflies found struggling on the surface.

Even if she escapes, many of her eggs are eaten by fish. Those laid in plant stems are attacked by parasitic wasps. The female wasp drills a hole in each egg and lays one of her own inside. The wasp egg hatches into a tiny larva, which feeds on the dragonfly egg. It quickly matures into a winged adult wasp and bites its way out of the stem.

However, enough eggs survive to provide large numbers of larvae. These are also eaten by fish. Other larvae fall prey to insects like the water-scorpion, which has special hooked legs for catching prey. It pierces the larva and sucks out the body juices. Some larvae fight back

These pondskaters are feeding on a dying damselfly that has fallen into the water.

using their tail-spines. The tip of the abdomen is curved around and thrust at the attacker. Others escape by breaking off a trapped leg. A new one grows later.

Enemies of Larvae and Adults

When the larva climbs out of the water just before it becomes an adult, the danger of being eaten increases. Only a small number of them will survive. Once each larva has fixed itself to a stem, it is easily seen but cannot run away. This is why many kinds of larvae come out at night, when there are fewer predators like birds around.

Many of those that come out in the day are seized by birds. They are often used to feed the birds' growing young. Many larvae are eaten by adult dragonflies. In tropical areas crocodiles snap up large numbers.

The surviving adults are at risk from birds, spiders and other insects. Larger dragonflies commonly pounce on the smaller, weaker damselflies.

A damselfly caught by a spider.

These are also more easily caught by web-spinning spiders. The larger dragonflies can break out of the web. Both types of insects may be attacked by hornets or wasps while they are resting. They are chewed up and fed to the wasp larvae.

Even plants can be dangerous. The sundew baits a sticky trap that insects find very attractive. They become firmly stuck to the trap and die. The plant absorbs the nitrogen from their dead bodies. This allows it to live in poor soil where other plants cannot thrive.

A spotted flycatcher snaps up a dragonfly in midair.

Dragonflies, Damselflies and Humans

Early Chinese and Japanese writings show that humans have been interested in these beautiful insects for centuries. Many poems were written praising dragonflies. They are often shown in delicate Japanese paintings. In parts of South America they are dried and used as nose ornaments. They are trapped in Malaysia using sticky twigs and eaten as a delicacy.

Some American Indians believe dragonflies to be the souls of the dead. They treat them with respect. In Japan, one kind of dragonfly is believed to carry the souls of the dead on visits to their families. Another name for Japan is Dragonfly Island.

Elsewhere they have not always been looked upon so kindly. The larvae can occasionally become a problem on fish farms. If there are large numbers of larvae they may eat too many young fish. In North America, some kinds of dragonflies feed on honeybees. They may damage the hive by killing large numbers of worker bees.

A Japanese plate is decorated with dragonflies.

The activities of humans can be very harmful to damselflies and dragonflies. To grow crops, people drain the wet places where they breed. The larvae can only live in very

Dragonfly larvae can cause trouble in fisheries by eating young fish.

clean water, but water is often poisoned with chemical waste.

5
Studying Damselflies and Dragonflies

The most likely place to find a beautiful damselfly like this is by a lake or near a pond.

The best place to study damselflies and dragonflies is in their natural **habitat**. If there is a shallow pond near your home, keep notes on the different kinds you find there and what they do. Always remember that ponds can be dangerous places. Many children drown every year. Always tell your parents when you are going to visit a pond.

If you have a yard, you can build your own pond there. In the past, ponds were made by "puddling." The bottom of the pond was built up using layers of straw and clay. This kept the water from draining away. Nowadays, people often use a plastic pond base. It does not matter which kind of pond you build, but it must have a shallow edge and lots of water weeds. The fully-grown larvae must be able to crawl out of the water.

If you have an aquarium, you can collect some larvae from a pond and watch them grow. Try not to disturb the pond too much. You must give the larvae plenty of food or they will attack each other. Pond insects, like mosquito larvae, and small fish, like sticklebacks, will do.

When the adults emerge, they should be set free. Adult dragonflies and damselflies are not easy to keep and will soon die in captivity.

This picture shows how the pond should slope at the sides. Plant pondweed at the bottom, rushes at the sides.

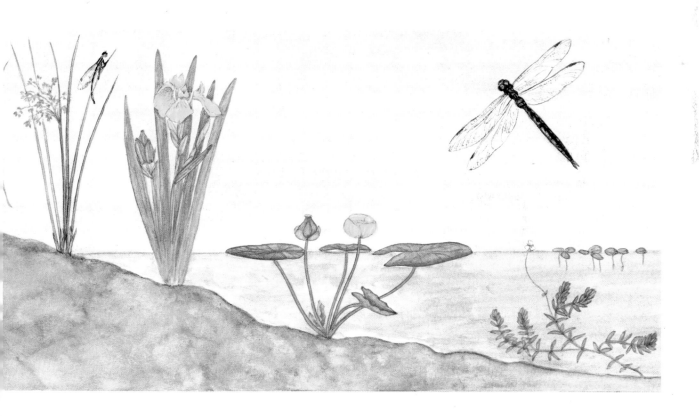

Glossary

Abdomen The rear of the three body parts of an insect, containing the intestine and sex organs.

Antennae The two feelers on the head of an insect that contain the sense of smell and touch.

Claspers A two-pronged tail at the tip of the male abdomen used to pick up the female during mating.

Compound eye The eye of most insects, made up of hundreds or thousands of separate visual units.

Courtship The way in which male and female animals behave toward one another prior to mating.

Exoskeleton The tough outer skin of an insect.

Facets The individual visual units that make up a compound eye.

Fossils The remains of an animal or plant that have been preserved in rock.

Gills The branched or feather-like structures used for breathing underwater.

Habitat The natural living place of a plant or animal.

Instar One of the stages an insect passes through during its growth.

In tandem A male and female damselfly or dragonfly held together as a pair in flight.

Larva (plural larvae) The form of an insect that emerges from the egg.

Mating The way in which male and female animals join together so that the female's eggs are fertilized by the male's sperm.

Ovipositor The egg-laying tube of a female insect.

Parasites Animals or plants that live and feed on others.

Predators Animals that hunt and kill other animals for food.

Pupa The stage in the growth of an insect when the larva is broken down and re-formed into the adult.

Rectum The lower part of an animal's gut through which waste is passed out of the body.

Siphon A tube-like growth of the body through which many water-living insects breathe.

Sperm The male sex cells used to fertilize a female's eggs.

Spiracles Breathing holes in the sides of an insect's abdomen and thorax that connect with a fine network of tubes taking oxygen to all parts of the body.

Thorax The middle part of an insect's body, bearing the legs and wings.

Finding Out More

You can find out more about dragonflies and damselflies by reading the following books:

Butterflies and Moths around the World by Eveline Jourdan. Lerner Publications, 1981.

A Complete Guide to British Dragonflies by Andrew McGeeney. Merrimack, 1986.

Dragonflies by Hidetoma Oda. Raintree Publishers, 1986.

Dragonflies by Cynthia Overbeck. Lerner Publications, 1982.

Good Bugs and Bag Bugs in Your Garden: Backyard Ecology. By Dorothy C. Hogner Crowell Junior Books, 1974.

Insects by Casey Horton. Franklin Watts, 1984.

Insects Do the Strangest Things by Leonora and Arthur Hornblow. Random House, 1968.

Insects You Have Seen by Lloyd Eighme. Review and Herald, 1980.

The Life of Insects by Maurice Burton. Silver, 1979.

Look at Insects rev. ed., by Rena K. Kirkpatrick. Raintree, 1985.

Our Six-Legged Friends and Allies: Ecology in your Back Yard by Hilda Simon. Vanguard, 1972.

Index

Picture Acknowledgments

All photographs from Oxford Scientific Films by the following photographers: A.C. Allnutt 23; G.I. Bernard 11 (left), 16, 17(left), 20, 25, 26, 28, 29 (left), 30, 31, 32, 33 (left and right), 36, 38; Raymond Blythe 13 (left); British Museum 9; J.A.L. Cooke 15, 29 (right); Stephen Dalton 27 (left), 39, 41; Bob Fredrick 27 (right); Tom Leach *cover, frontispiece,* 10, 13 (right), 21, 34, 42; G.A. MacLean 12, 35; Mantis Wildlife Films 18; Alastair Shay 14, 17 (right), 22 (left & right), 24, 37; Lynn M. Stone 8; David Thompson 11 (right); P & W Ward 19; Ronald Sheridan Collection 40. Illustration on page 43 by Vanda Baginska.